BOTSWANA: HUMAN RIGHTS

EXECUTIVE SUMMARY

Botswana has been a constitutional multi-party republican democracy since independence in 1966. Its constitution provides for the indirect election of a president and the popular election of a national assembly. In 2009 the ruling Botswana Democratic Party (BDP) won the majority of parliamentary seats in an election deemed generally free and fair. President Ian Khama, who has held the presidency since the resignation of former president Festus Mogae in 2008, retained his position. The BDP has held the presidency and a majority of National Assembly seats since independence. Security forces reported to civilian authorities. Authorities maintained effective control over the security forces. Security forces sometimes committed human rights abuses.

Violence, including sexual violence, against women and children; child labor in cattle herding, agriculture, and other work; and discrimination against the Basarwa people persisted as principal human rights concerns.

Other significant human rights problems included occasional excessive use of force and abuse by security personnel, police corruption, government attempts to limit press freedom, and shortcomings in the judicial process including lengthy delays and failure to inform defendants of their pretrial rights. Societal problems included trafficking in persons and discrimination against women and children; persons with disabilities; persons with HIV/AIDS; and gay, lesbian, bisexual, and transgender (LGBT) persons.

The government took steps to prosecute officials who committed abuses, including prosecuting and convicting military officers for murder. Impunity was generally not a problem.

Section 1. Respect for the Integrity of the Person, Including Freedom from:

a. Arbitrary or Unlawful Deprivation of Life

There were no reports the government or its agents committed an unlawful killing during the reporting year. In July 2012 Botswana Defence Force (BDF) soldiers shot and killed two suspected poachers who entered the country illegally from Namibia. The case was under police investigation at year's end. There is no independent government body charged with investigating security force killings.

b. Disappearance

There were no reports of politically motivated disappearances.

c. Torture and Other Cruel, Inhuman, or Degrading Treatment or Punishment

The constitution and law prohibit such practices. There was one report that security force personnel abused an inmate during the reporting year.

Prison and Detention Center Conditions

Prison and detention center conditions generally met international standards, and the government permitted visits by independent human rights observers. Prison and detention center conditions improved during the year with further reduction of inmate overcrowding. The inmate population declined to below recommended capacity in the country's 22 prisons and one detention center for irregular immigrants.

Physical Conditions: As of October the prison system held 4,124 inmates against its authorized capacity of 4,337. As of September there were 211 juvenile prisoners, including 210 males and one female. Authorities held pretrial detainees and convicts separately, and juveniles occasionally were held with adults but only for a few days while awaiting transport. Authorities allowed mothers to bring their nursing babies under the age of two with them into the prison system, some of which lacked maternity facilities. In instances where a child is above two years in age, and if no family is available to take care of the child, nongovernmental organizations (NGOs) care for the child until release of the mother. Conditions for men and women prisoners were comparable.

In 2012 there were three deaths in prisons and pretrial detention centers. Prisons and overnight jails provided drinking water. There was adequate food, sanitation, ventilation, and lighting in prisons. Prisoners received access to basic medical care. As of September, 964 inmates were tested for HIV, including 763 citizens and 201 noncitizens. Of those, 88 citizen prisoners and 36 noncitizen prisoners tested HIV-positive. HIV-positive citizen prisoners received free antiretroviral drugs and blood counts, specimen collection, and viral load monitoring. These services were not free for noncitizen HIV-positive prisoners. The government, however, provided voluntary, free HIV testing and peer counseling through infectious disease control centers located within the prison precincts for both citizen and noncitizen prisoners. In addition, its programs of voluntary, safe male circumcision and prevention of mother-to-child transmission of HIV to reduce the spread of new HIV/AIDS infections were available to all prisoners. As of September, 79 male inmates underwent circumcision, including 56 citizens and 23 noncitizens.

Administration: Prison recordkeeping was adequate but mostly utilized paper records, and there was no plan to upgrade to computerized systems. The prison commissioner had the authority to release terminally ill prisoners in the last 12 months of their sentences and to allow citizen prisoners with sentences of 12 months or less to complete their sentences outside the prison by completing an "extramural" work release program at government facilities. Eligible prisoners must have served short-term sentences with at least half of their sentences completed and must not have been previously incarcerated. Prisoners convicted of violent and other serious felonies were ineligible. As of September authorities released 327 prisoners to complete their sentences through extramural labor.

Prisoners and detainees had access to visitors, including foreign government representatives, and authorities permitted religious observance. Inmates could file uncensored complaints directly to judicial authorities or through a prisoner ombudsman. Authorities investigated allegations brought by inmates against prison officials and took disciplinary or judicial action against persons responsible for abuses. Officers of the courts, including magistrates and judges, regularly conducted visits to prisons to check on prison conditions. Although they are required by law to visit prisons on a quarterly basis, government-appointed welfare and oversight committees did not visit prisons during the year.

Independent Monitoring: The government allowed access to citizen and noncitizen prisoners by international and local NGOs. The International Committee of the Red Cross visited prison facilities and representatives of the Office of the United Nations High Commissioner for Refugees (UNHCR) visited the Center for Illegal Immigrants in Francistown during the year.

d. Arbitrary Arrest or Detention

The constitution and law prohibit arbitrary arrest and detention and the government generally observed these prohibitions. The Directorate for Intelligence and Security (DIS) detained a citizen overnight based on an overheard political comment that DIS claimed an agent interpreted as a threat to the president. He was released the following day.

Role of the Police and Security Apparatus

The Botswana Police Service (BPS), under the Ministry of Defense, Justice, and Security in the Office of the President, has primary responsibility for internal security. The army, which reports to the president through the presidentially appointed Defense Council and its commanding general, an ex officio member of the council, is responsible for external security and has some domestic security responsibilities. DIS is under the Office of the President. It collects and evaluates external and internal intelligence, provides personal protection to high-level government officials, and advises the presidency and government on matters of national security. Civilian authorities maintained effective control over the BPS, army, and DIS, and the government had effective mechanisms to investigate and punish abuse and corruption. There were no reports of impunity involving security forces during the year.

During the year 37 BPS officers received human rights training at the International Law Enforcement Academy located in the country.

Arrest Procedures and Treatment of Detainees

Police officers must produce an arrest warrant issued by a duly authorized magistrate upon the presentation of compelling evidence, except in certain cases, such as when an officer witnesses a crime being committed or discovers a suspect is in possession of a controlled substance. DIS personnel have the power to enter premises and make arrests without warrants if the agency suspects a person has committed or is about to commit a crime. Elements of civil society continued to criticize DIS, claiming it did not receive sufficient independent oversight and posed a potential threat to civil liberties.

The law requires authorities to inform suspects of their rights upon arrest, including the right to remain silent, and to file charges before a magistrate within 48 hours. Authorities generally respected these rights. There were no reports during the year of denial of a suspect's right to an attorney during the first 48 hours after arrest and arraignment before a magistrate. A magistrate may order a suspect held for 14 days through a writ of detention, which may be renewed every 14 days. The law provides for a prompt judicial determination of the legality of a person's detention. Heavy court caseloads occasionally delayed this determination.

Authorities generally informed detainees of the reason for their detention, although there were some complaints this did not always occur. There is a functioning bail system, and detention without bail was unusual except in murder cases, where it is mandatory. Detainees have the right to contact a family member and hire attorneys of their choice; however, most could not afford legal counsel. In capital cases the government provides legal counsel or private attorneys work pro bono for indigent clients. Courts tried those charged with noncapital crimes without legal representation if they could not afford an attorney. There were no reports during the year of suspects being held incommunicado or under house arrest.

Pretrial Detention: The law provides for a prompt judicial determination of the legality of a person's detention. A writ of pretrial detention is for 14 days and is renewable every 14 days. Some detainees waited from several weeks to several months between the filing of charges and the start of their trials. As of September, 1,000 of the 4,059 persons in custody were pretrial detainees. Pretrial detention in murder, rape, livestock theft, and robbery cases sometimes lasted beyond one year, but there were no reports of instances in which the length of detention equaled or exceeded the sentences. Such delays were largely due to judicial staffing shortages.

e. Denial of Fair Public Trial

The constitution and law provide for an independent judiciary and the government generally respected judicial independence. The civil courts remained unable to provide timely trials due to severe staffing shortages and a backlog of pending cases. Trials are open to the public.

In addition to the civil court system, a customary or traditional court system also exists. According to traditional practice, a tribal chief presides over most small villages. Small claims courts were established in 2009 in Francistown, Gaborone, and some surrounding areas, but there were reports of heavy caseloads and new procedures limiting the courts' effectiveness. Many cases remained delayed for several months, and the National Legal Association criticized judges who did not deliver rulings in a timely manner. In October the chief justice alleged some judges might have accepted bribes from forum-shopping lawyers. The association refuted the allegations, claiming there was no evidence judges accepted bribes. The association conceded, however, that forum shopping occasionally occurred, as lawyers sought out judges known for making timely decisions, rather than those who did not.

Trial Procedures

The constitution and law provide for the right to a fair trial, and an independent judiciary generally enforced this right. Defendants enjoy a presumption of innocence. Trials in the civil courts are public, although trials under the National Security Act may be secret. There is no jury system. Defendants have the right to be present and consult with an attorney in a timely manner, but the state provides an attorney only in capital cases. As a result, many defendants were not aware of their procedural rights as they relate to pretrial or trial proceedings. Defendants may question witnesses against them and have access to government-held evidence relevant to their cases. Defendants may present witnesses and evidence on their own behalf. Defendants have the right to appeal and to adequate time and facilities to prepare their defense. Defendants are not compelled to testify or confess guilt. The constitution states these rights extend to all citizens. Some NGOs provided limited, free legal assistance.

While customary or traditional courts enjoy widespread citizen support and respect, they often did not afford the same due process protections as the formal court system. Although defendants may confront, question, and present witnesses in customary court proceedings, they do not have legal counsel, and there are no standardized rules of evidence. Customary trials are open to the public, and defendants may present evidence on their own behalf. Tribal judges, appointed by the tribal leader or elected by the community, determine sentences. Many tribal judges were poorly trained. The quality of decisions reached in the customary courts varied considerably, and defendants often lacked a presumption of innocence. Tribal judge sentences applied corporal punishment such as lashings on the buttocks more often than did civil court sentences. Those convicted in customary courts may file appeals through the civil court system.

There is a separate military court system, which does not try civilians. Military courts have separate procedures from civil courts. Defendants in military courts are able to retain private attorneys at their own expense and see the evidence slated to be used against them.

Political Prisoners and Detainees

There were no reports of political prisoners or detainees.

Civil Judicial Procedures and Remedies

In the formal judicial system, there is an independent and impartial judiciary in civil matters, including for human rights cases, which includes a separate industrial court for most labor-related cases. Administrative remedies were not widely available. By mutual agreement of the parties involved, most civil cases were tried in customary courts, which handle land, marital, and property disputes and often do not afford due process.

f. Arbitrary Interference with Privacy, Family, Home, or Correspondence

The constitution and law prohibit such actions, and the government generally respected these prohibitions. The government's continued narrow interpretation of a 2006 High Court ruling, however, resulted in a few hundred indigenous Basarwa people (also called the San) being prohibited from living or hunting in their tribal homeland, the Central Kalahari Game Reserve (CKGR). Although authorities permitted some of the original residents to return to the CKGR, their children and other relatives continue to be required to have permits to come and go from the CKGR. Government officials maintained the resettlement program was voluntary and necessary to facilitate the delivery of public services, provide socioeconomic development opportunities to the Basarwa, and minimize human impact on wildlife. In May 2012 the Basarwa appealed to the UN Permanent Forum on Indigenous Issues, asking the United Nations to force the government to recognize their land and resource rights. The forum approved a set of nine draft recommendations addressing the impact of land seizures and government disenfranchisement of indigenous people. In August attorneys for the Basarwa people filed a High Court case in which the original complainants from the 2006 CKGR case appealed to government for unrestricted access to the CKGR for their children and relatives (i.e. without permits). The case was dismissed for technical reasons, with permission given by the court to refile with a new application.

Government relocations continued during the year in the Ranyane settlement and, in May, the High Court ruled the government must stop relocating families from the settlement. NGOs reported the government continued its relocations, despite the court ruling. In June the High Court issued a restraining order prohibiting the government from relocating residents from the Ranyane settlement.

The government denied allegations of forced resettlements and claimed that many Ranyane residents expressed a desire for relocation assistance so they would have better access to government schools, medical facilities, and other accommodations not available at Ranyane. The case was pending at year's end.

Section 2. Respect for Civil Liberties, Including:

a. Freedom of Speech and Press

The constitution and law provide for freedom of speech and press, and the government generally respected freedom of speech. The law restricts freedom of speech of some government officials and provides for fines against persons found guilty of insulting public officials or national symbols. The law states, "Any person in a public place or at a public gathering (who) uses abusive, obscene or insulting language in relation to the President, any other member of the National Assembly or any public officer" is guilty of an offense and may be fined up 400 pula ($47). The penal code also states that any person who insults the country's arms, flag, presidential standard, or national anthem is guilty of an offense and may be fined up to 500 pula ($58). The Media Institute of Southern Africa (MISA) and other NGOs reported the government attempted to limit press freedom and continued to dominate domestic broadcasting.

Press Freedoms: In 2008 Parliament passed the Media Practitioners Act, which established a Media Council to register and accredit journalists, promote ethical standards among the media, and receive public complaints. Some NGOs, including MISA, the independent media, and opposition members of parliament continued to criticize the law, stating it restricted press freedom and was passed without debate after consultations between the government and stakeholders collapsed. The act had yet to be implemented.

The government owned and operated the Botswana Press Agency, which dominated the print media through its free, nationally distributed newspaper, *Daily News*, and two state-operated FM radio stations. State-owned media generally featured reporting favorable to the government and were susceptible to political interference. Opposition political parties claimed state media coverage heavily favored the ruling party.

The independent media were active and generally expressed a wide variety of views, which frequently included strong criticism of the government; however, members of the media complained they were sometimes subject to government pressure to portray the government and the country in a positive light. It was sometimes more difficult for private media organizations than for government-owned ones to obtain access to government-held information.

Censorship or Content Restrictions: Some members of civil society organizations alleged the government occasionally censored stories in the government-run media it deemed undesirable. Government journalists sometimes practiced self-censorship.

Internet Freedom

There were no government restrictions on access to the internet or credible reports the government monitored e-mail or internet chat rooms. According to the World Bank, in 2012, 11.5 percent of individuals used the internet.

Academic Freedom and Cultural Events

There were no government restrictions on academic freedom or cultural events.

b. Freedom of Peaceful Assembly and Association

The constitution and law provide for freedom of assembly and association, and the government generally respected these rights.

c. Freedom of Religion

See the Department of State's *International Religious Freedom Report* at www.state.gov/j/drl/irf/rpt.

d. Freedom of Movement, Internally Displaced Persons, Protection of Refugees, and Stateless Persons

The constitution and law provide for freedom of internal movement, foreign travel, emigration, and repatriation, and the government generally respected these rights.

In-country Movement: In 2011 the Court of Appeals awarded the Basarwa the right to reopen or drill new boreholes to gain access to water for domestic use. Prior to the ruling, the government banned the Basarwa from accessing wells, which prevented them from returning home to the CKGR. Following the ruling, the government granted the appropriate permits for workers and machinery to enter the CKGR to drill boreholes. With funding from international advocacy groups and a local diamond mining company, the Basarwa were able to access water through a borehole. According to a case study published in June 2012 by Minority Rights Group International, *Basarwa Evicted over Diamonds*, Gope mine owner,

Gem Diamonds, was to work with CKGR residents in order that they would benefit from the mine. Gem was to drill four new boreholes, hire residents, and establish a community trust, but only one waterhole had been drilled by year's end.

Protection of Refugees

Access to Asylum: The law provides for the granting of asylum or refugee status, and the government has established a system for providing protection to refugees. The government's system for granting refugee status was accessible but slow. The government provided protection against the expulsion or return of persons to countries where their lives or freedom would be threatened on account of their race, religion, nationality, membership in a particular social group, or political opinion.

The government cooperated with UNHCR and other humanitarian organizations in assisting more than 3,500 refugees and asylum seekers. During the year refugee status was granted to seven persons. The government held newly arrived refugees and asylum seekers, primarily from Zimbabwe, in the Center for Illegal Immigrants in Francistown until the Refugee Advisory Committee, a governmental body whose chairperson is the district commissioner of Francistown, made a status recommendation. UNHCR representatives participated in advisory committee meetings as observers and technical advisers. Having granted refugee status, the government transferred the individuals in question to the Dukwe Refugee Camp.

Refugee applicants who were unsuccessful in obtaining asylum also were allowed to remain at Dukwe if they wished pending deportation or voluntary repatriation. In 2012 following UNHCR's revocation of refugee status for 43 people, the government gave notice it intended to start deportation proceedings. During the year UNHCR reassessed the cases and found that only 15 of the 43applicants failed to meet the criteria for refugee status. As of October the 15 individuals denied refugee status had not been deported.

Employment: As of October almost all of the country's 2,796 registered refugees and 284 registered asylum seekers were living and working in and around Dukwe. There were also 428 former Angolan refugees whose refugee status was revoked and who were awaiting voluntary repatriation at Dukwe. The government stated that as a general policy, all registered refugees must reside in the Dukwe camp, although it may permit residence outside the camp in exceptional cases, such as for refugees enrolled at a university or with unique skills.

Access to Basic Services: Refugees in Dukwe had access to education and health care. UNHCR facilitates refugee and asylum seeker exit permit applications for medical referrals as necessary. Exit permits are typically granted for three days and if refugees are found outside the camp without a permit, they may be arrested. Although asylum seekers were not housed with irregular immigrants, the UNHCR criticized the detention of asylum seekers at the Center for Illegal Immigrants because, according to international law, asylum seekers should not be held in detention facilities. The UNHCR reported conditions at the center were poor and it continued to monitor treatment of detainees at the center during the year. Children in the center did not have sufficient access to education during their detention. Refugees and asylum seekers, including women, unaccompanied minors, elderly persons, and pregnant and lactating mothers, were kept alongside illegal immigrants and those accused of criminal activity. Detention periods were generally of short duration, but in some cases lasted several months and differed depending on a detainee's nationality.

Durable Solutions: In August 2012 the UNHCR announced a voluntary repatriation program for an estimated 1,000 Namibian refugees to their native Caprivi Strip. As of June the UNHCR reported that 29 Namibian refugees had returned.

In July the government, following UNHCR policy guidance, announced the cessation of refugee status for Angolan refugees in the country and stated that it would work with the UNHCR to repatriate voluntarily all Angolans by the end of October. The government issued a notice that any Angolan not accepting voluntarily repatriation would be considered an illegal immigrant after November 30.

Temporary Protection: In 2012 the government provided temporary protection at Dukwe to 57 individuals who may not qualify as refugees under the 1951 UN refugee convention or the 1967 protocol. The UNHCR provided food and other provisions to individuals under temporary protection.

Section 3. Respect for Political Rights: The Right of Citizens to Change Their Government

The constitution and law provide citizens the right to change their government peacefully, and citizens exercised this right through periodic, free, and fair elections based on universal suffrage.

Elections and Political Participation

Recent Elections: In 2009 the ruling BDP won the majority of National Assembly seats in a general election deemed by international and domestic observers to be generally free and fair. President Ian Khama retained the presidency, which he has held since 2008.

Participation of Women and Minorities: There were five women in the 61-seat National Assembly, one of whom was the speaker and four of whom served in the 24-member cabinet. There were also three women in the expanded 35-seat House of Chiefs.

While the constitution formally recognizes eight principal tribes of the Tswana nation, amendments to the constitution also allow minority tribes to be represented in the expanded House of Chiefs. Under the law members from all groups enjoy equal rights, and minority tribes have representation that is at least equal to that of the eight principal tribes.

Section 4. Corruption and Lack of Transparency in Government

The law provides criminal penalties for corruption by officials, and the government generally sought to implement these laws effectively. The authorities tasked with enforcement were undertrained and underresourced. There were isolated reports of government corruption during the year.

Corruption: In 2012 police initiated investigations into corruption charges against four police officers, who were found guilty and dismissed. Also 31 officers were dismissed for failure to adhere to the code of conduct; of these, three were charged with criminal offenses and 28 were charged with disciplinary offenses. Police officials acknowledged corruption was a problem in the lower ranks and some officers took advantage of irregular immigrants and traffic violators by exacting bribes.

The Parliamentary Committee on Statutory Bodies is responsible for the oversight of state-owned enterprises and all government bodies. The committee was active and during the year released several reports relating to alleged mismanagement in certain state-owned enterprises, including Air Botswana and Botswana Railways.

The law requires the Auditor General's Office to submit an annual government audit report, and it did so in a timely manner. A law enacted in 2012 brought the

Auditor General's Office under the Office of the President and made the auditor general's position a presidentially appointed one.

The Directorate on Corruption and Economic Crime (DCEC) and the Financial Intelligence Agency (FIA) are responsible for combating corruption. The DCEC is an autonomous law enforcement agency established by law to combat corruption through investigation, prevention, and education. Following investigation, it submits its findings to the Directorate of Public Prosecutions (DPP). Media and civil society observers viewed the DCEC and the DPP as insufficiently resourced to combat high-level or sophisticated corruption schemes.

In 2012 the DCEC received 1,646 reports of fraud, corruption, economic crime, and money laundering. There were 1,476 active investigations during the year, including carryovers from previous years. The most common types of allegations were illegal land acquisition, abuse of office, bribery, conflicts of interest, and illegal acquisition of documents such as work and residence permits, visas, and driver's licenses. The media reported on investigations into allegations of corruption and financial mismanagement at the Botswana Meat Commission, Botswana Power Corporation, and Botswana Development Corporation. The investigations continued during the year.

The FIA is not an investigative organ and has no police powers. Once fully operational, the FIA is to collect, analyze, interpret, and disseminate financial information to identify potential domestic and international criminal activity, including money laundering and terrorist financing. The minister of finance and development planning appoints the director of the FIA, but the organization was not fully staffed or operational by year's end. In April the Eastern and Southern Africa Anti-Money Laundering Group cited the country as not being in full compliance with Financial Action Task Force standards, in part because of the minister's failure to issue regulations that would allow the FIA to become fully operational.

Whistleblower Protection: The law does not specifically provide protection to public and private employees for making internal disclosures or lawful public disclosures of evidence of illegality.

Financial Disclosure: There are no formal financial disclosure laws; however, in 2009, a presidential directive required all cabinet ministers to declare their interests, assets, and liabilities to the president. Critics contended that this policy did not go far enough to promote transparency and that financial declarations by senior government officials should be available to the public.

Public Access to Information: The law does not provide public access to government information and the government generally restricted such access. The Government Printing Office releases information that is made available to the public for a fee. In August 2012 the National Assembly voted down an opposition Freedom of Information bill.

Section 5. Governmental Attitude Regarding International and Nongovernmental Investigation of Alleged Violations of Human Rights

A number of domestic and international human rights groups generally operated without government restriction, investigating and publishing their findings on human rights cases. Government officials were generally cooperative and responsive to domestic NGO views on most subjects. The government interacted with and provided financial support to some domestic organizations.

Government Human Rights Bodies: An autonomous ombudsman handled complaints of maladministration and violation of human rights in the public sector and the government generally cooperated with the ombudsman. The office suffered from a shortage of staff and some criticized its effectiveness. Public awareness of the office and its services was low. It reported 18 cases of alleged police torture between 2006 and 2011, of which two were referred to the DPP for prosecution. The ombudsman determined there was insufficient evidence to justify referring the 16 remaining cases for prosecution.

Section 6. Discrimination, Societal Abuses, and Trafficking in Persons

The constitution and law prohibit governmental discrimination based on ethnicity, race, nationality, creed, sex, or social status, and the government generally respected these provisions. In addition, as long as a government job applicant is able to perform the duties of the position, he or she may not be discriminated against due to disability or language. The law does not prohibit discrimination by private persons or entities, however, and there was societal discrimination against women; persons with disabilities; minority ethnic groups, particularly the San; LGBT persons; persons with HIV/AIDS; and persons with albinism.

Women

Rape and Domestic Violence: The law criminalizes rape but does not recognize spousal rape as a crime. Laws against rape were effectively enforced when victims pressed charges; however, police noted victims often declined to press charges against the perpetrators, and the extent of the problem was likely underreported. In some cases of domestic nonspousal rape, victims were afraid of losing financial support if perpetrators were found guilty and imprisoned. NGOs continued efforts to improve awareness of the crime. By law the minimum sentence for rape is 10 years in prison, increasing to 15 years with corporal punishment if the offender is HIV-positive, and 20 years with corporal punishment if the offender was aware of having HIV-positive status. By law formal courts try all rape cases. A person convicted of rape is required to undergo an HIV test before sentencing. The BPS did not have a specific unit dedicated to rape investigation but had trained crime scene investigators and a forensics unit to respond to cases of rape and domestic violence.

The law prohibits domestic and other violence, whether against women or men, but it remained a serious problem. Police released the following domestic violence statistics for the first nine months of 2012: five cases of incest; 375 of defilement; 102 of indecent assault on females, although those sexual assault cases reported were believed to represent only a fraction of the actual number of such incidents; 73 reported cases of passion killings; and 589 death threats. Greater public awareness resulted in increased reporting of domestic violence and sexual assault.

Sexual Harassment: The law prohibits sexual harassment in both the private and public sectors. Sexual harassment committed by a public officer is considered misconduct and punishable by termination, potentially with forfeiture of all retirement benefits; suspension with loss of pay and benefits for up to three months; reduction in rank or pay; deferment or stoppage of a pay raise; or reprimand. Nonetheless, sexual harassment continued to be a widespread problem, particularly by men in positions of authority, including teachers and supervisors. In 2012 the minister of presidential affairs and public administration, along with the Gender Affairs Department in the Ministry of Labor and Home Affairs and local government officials, announced plans to begin a campaign to address sexual harassment in the public sector but had not begun implementation by year's end.

Reproductive Rights: Couples and individuals have the right to decide freely and responsibly the number, spacing, and timing of their children and to have the information and means to do so free from discrimination, coercion, and violence. Family planning services were widely available, and the United Nations reported 51 percent of women and girls ages 15-49 used a modern method of contraception in 2011. According to UN estimates, skilled health personnel attended 99 percent of births in the country as a whole, with lower rates in rural areas. The Ministry of Health reported 90 percent of births took place in hospitals, where obstetric care was widely available. A government program, Prevention of Mother-to-Child Transmission of HIV, effectively reduced mother-to-child transmission. According to the United Nations Population Fund, the maternal mortality rate was 160 deaths per 100,000 live births in 2010, with 56 percent of those deaths related to HIV and AIDS. The Ministry of Health reported 90 percent of births took place in hospitals. The leading causes of maternal mortality include post-partum hemorrhage, hypertensive disorders of pregnancy, abortion, and HIV/AIDS-related infections. The major factors hindering greater contraceptive prevalence rates include a shortage of supplies, provider biases, inadequately skilled health-care workers, HIV status, culture, religion, and popularly accepted myths and misconceptions.

Discrimination: By law women have the same civil rights as men, but societal discrimination persisted. The country has a dual legal system consisting of formal law derived from the constitution and customary law based on tribal practice. A number of traditional laws enforced by tribal structures and customary courts restricted women's property rights and economic opportunities, particularly in rural areas. Marriages may occur under one of three systems, each with its own implications for women's property rights. A woman married under traditional law or in "common property" is held to be a legal minor and required to have her husband's consent to buy or sell property, apply for credit, and enter into legally binding contracts. Under an intermediate system referred to as "in community of property," married women may own real estate and other property in their own names, and the law stipulates neither spouse may dispose of joint property without the written consent of the other. Women increasingly exercised the right to marriage "out of common property," in which they retained their full legal rights as adults. Polygamy is legal under traditional law with the consent of the first wife but was not common. In October 2012 the High Court ruled gender discrimination based on customary law was unconstitutional. The court found in favor of three sisters who challenged Ngawaketse customary law giving rights of inheritance to the youngest son. In September an appeals court upheld the 2012 decision.

Skilled urban women had increasing access to entry and mid-level white-collar jobs. According to a 2007 Grant Thornton International Business Report, 74 percent of businesses employed women in senior management positions, while women occupied 31 percent of such positions. Women occupied many senior-level positions in government bodies. These included speaker of the national assembly, governor of the Bank of Botswana, attorney general, ministers of trade and industry and of education and skills development, assistant ministers of local government and health, the ombudsman, and numerous permanent secretary positions. Nevertheless, a Southern African Development Community (SADC) study, *Gender Protocol 2012 Barometer-Botswana,* reported women's representation was 21 percent of cabinet ministers, 8 percent of parliamentarians, and 19.4 percent of local government councilors. The study found that more than 60 percent of local government employees were women. In 2008 the BDF began to admit women. In 2011 four women completed flight training and became BDF pilots. In October 2012 the BDF announced it would begin recruiting women in the enlisted ranks, where previously women could enter only as officer cadets, but had not begun doing so at year's end.

The Gender Affairs Department in the Ministry of Labor and Home Affairs has responsibility for promoting and protecting women's rights and welfare. The department provided grants to NGOs working on women's issues. The SADC study found that women owned and operated the majority of informal sector businesses, but the proportion of women in salaried formal employment was lower than that of men. There is no legal requirement that women receive equal pay for equal work.

Children

Birth Registration: In general, citizenship is derived from one's parents, although there are very limited circumstances in which citizenship may be derived from birth within the country's territory. The government generally registered births promptly; however, there were some delays in remote locations. Unregistered children may be denied some government services.

Education: Education was not compulsory. School fees and uniform and book costs had to be covered by parents but could be waived for children whose family income fell below a certain amount.

Child Abuse: Child abuse occurred and was often reported to police in cases of physical harm to a child. Police referred the children and, depending on the level of abuse, their alleged abuser(s) to counseling in the Department of Social Services as well as to local NGOs. Some cases were referred to the Attorney General's Office for prosecution. Local human rights groups raised concerns about the use and administration of corporal punishment by traditional courts and in schools, which many believed to be excessive.

Forced and Early Marriage: Child marriage occurred infrequently and was largely limited to certain tribes. The government does not recognize marriages that occur when either party is under the minimum legal age of 18.

Sexual Exploitation of Children: The Children's Act of 2010 prohibits the prostitution and sexual abuse of children. Sex with a child younger than 16 constitutes defilement and is punishable by a minimum of 10 years' incarceration. Police reported 375 cases of defilement and five cases of incest through the end of September 2012. There were defilement investigations and convictions during the year. There were reports teachers sexually abused students. Reports indicated that children occasionally were sexually abused by extended family members with whom they lived.

By law child prostitution is an act of defilement punishable by a minimum of 10 years' imprisonment. Child pornography is a criminal offense punishable by five to 15 years in prison. Media and NGO reports claimed that prostituted children were made available to truck drivers, mainly along the trucking route in the eastern region linking the country with South Africa, and that many of the girls and boys were thought to be orphans. As part of a project funded by the International Labor Organization (ILO), the children's rights NGO Childline reported removing 58 children from commercial sexual exploitation between August 2010 and January 2012. Children's rights NGO Humana People to People Botswana, working separately on the same ILO project, reported it removed two children from commercial sexual exploitation between June 2010 and May 2012

Displaced Children: In 2011 the United Nations Children's Fund estimated there were 150,000 orphans in the country, of which approximately 120,000 had lost one or both parents due to HIV/AIDS. As of July the government had registered 38,576 children as orphans and 32,068 as vulnerable. The government defines an orphan as a child both of whose parents are dead, while the United Nations defines an orphan as a child with one or both parents deceased.) Once registered as orphans, the children received school uniforms, shelter, a monthly food basket worth between 216 pula ($25) and 600 pula ($70), depending upon location, and counseling as needed. There were no reports of police abusing orphans.

International Child Abductions: The country is not a party to the 1980 Hague Convention on the Civil Aspects of International Child Abduction.

Anti-Semitism

The Jewish community was estimated to number 100 people. There were no reports of anti-Semitic acts.

Trafficking in Persons

See the Department of State's *Trafficking in Persons Report* at www.state.gov/j/tip.

Persons with Disabilities

The law prohibits discrimination against persons with physical and mental disabilities in education, employment, access to health care, or the provision of other state services. The law does not prohibit discrimination by private persons or entities. The law does not specifically prohibit discrimination against persons with sensory or intellectual disabilities. The government has a national policy that provides for integrating the needs of persons with disabilities into all aspects of government policymaking. The government mandates access to public buildings or transportation for persons with disabilities, but civil society sources reported that access for persons with disabilities was limited. The law does not specifically include air travel with other modes of transportation, but in general persons with disabilities were provided access to air transportation. Although new government buildings were being constructed to assure access by persons with disabilities, older government office buildings remained largely inaccessible. Most new privately owned buildings provided access for persons with disabilities.

There was some discrimination against persons with disabilities, and employment opportunities remained limited. Children with disabilities attended school, and there were no patterns of abuse in educational and mental health facilities. The government did not restrict persons with disabilities from voting or participating in civil affairs and made some accommodations during elections to allow for persons with disabilities to vote.

There is a department of disability coordination in the Office of the President to assist persons with disabilities. The Department of Labor is responsible for protecting the rights of persons with disabilities in the labor force and investigating claims of discrimination. Individuals may also bring cases directly to the Industrial Court. The government funded NGOs that provided rehabilitation services and supported small-scale projects for workers with disabilities.

Indigenous People

An estimated 50,000-60,000 people belong to one of the many scattered, diverse tribal groups known as Basarwa. The Baswarwa people constitute approximately 3 percent of the population and are culturally and linguistically distinct from most other residents. The law prohibits discrimination against the Basarwa with respect to employment, housing, health services, and cultural practices; however, the Basarwa remained marginalized economically and politically and generally did not have access to their traditional land. The Basarwa continued to be geographically isolated, had limited access to education, lacked adequate political representation, and were not fully aware of their civil rights. NGOs report forced labor of Basarwa people – including adults and children – on private farms and cattle posts.

While the government respected the 2006 High Court ruling on a suit filed by 189 Basarwa regarding their forced relocation, it continued to interpret the ruling to allow only the 189 actual applicants and their spouses and minor children to return to the CKGR. The court ruled the applicants were entitled to return to the CKGR without entry permits and to be issued permits to hunt in designated wildlife management areas, which are not located in the CKGR. The children and other family members of the original applicants were not permitted to return to the CKGR without entry permits. Many of the Basarwa and their supporters continued to object to the government's narrow interpretation of this ruling. Negotiations between San representatives and the government regarding residency and hunting rights stalled after the court ruling provided the right to access water.

In August attorneys for the Basarwa filed a High Court case in which the original complainants from the 2006 CKGR case appealed to the government for unrestricted access to the CKGR for their children and other relatives (i.e., permits not required). The case was dismissed for technical reasons, with permission given by the court to refile with a new application.

In a move criticized by civil society and local media, the government added the Basarwa applicants' lawyer, a United Kingdom citizen affiliated with Survival International, to a list of individuals from visa waiver countries who must apply for visas to enter the country. While the government denied allegations that it planned to bar the lawyer from the country, it did not grant his visa in time for him to participate in the August High Court hearing.

Government relocations continued during the year in the western settlement of Ranyane. On May 28, the High Court ruled the government must stop the relocation of families from the Ranyane settlement. NGOs reported that the government relocated 11 families from Ranyane after the High Court ruling and alleged that government officials installed themselves in Ranyane in order to conduct a campaign to induce residents to move from their village, in part by blocking access to the settlement's only water supply. In response to a complaint filed on behalf of residents, on June 18 the court issued a restraining order prohibiting the government from relocating residents from Ranyane and from blocking access to the water pipe, entering any household without occupants' permission, and removing residents without first notifying the community's lawyers.

The government denied allegations of forced resettlements and claimed many Ranyane residents expressed a desire for relocation assistance so they could have better access to government schools, medical facilities, and other accommodations not available at Ranyane.

During the year there were no government programs directly addressing discrimination against the Basarwa. With the exception of the 2006 court ruling, there were no demarcated cultural lands.

A number of NGOs made efforts to promote the rights of the Basarwa or to help provide economic opportunities. The programs had limited impact, however. The NGO Survival International, along with other independent organizations, continued to criticize the government decision to allow mining exploration in the CKGR. The NGOs argued diamond exploration in the CKGR would have a significant negative impact on the life and environment of the Basarwa.

In December 2012 police were accused of beating two Basarwa for allegedly hunting without a permit in the CKGR. According to Survival International, the Basarwa were fined and released.

During the year the government brought charges against six Basarwa CKGR residents for allegedly unlawful possession of hunted carcasses. The cases were pending at year's end.

Societal Abuses, Discrimination, and Acts of Violence Based on Sexual Orientation and Gender Identity

The law does not explicitly criminalize consensual same-sex sexual activity. What the law describes as "unnatural acts" are criminalized, and there was widespread belief this is directed toward LGBT persons. Police did not target persons suspected of same-sex sexual activity, and there were no reported cases during the year of violence against persons based on their sexual orientation or gender identity. LGBT-rights organizations claimed there were incidents of violence, societal harassment, and discrimination based on sexual orientation or gender identity, however. Civil society leaders reported that overt intimidation was not generally a factor in preventing reports of abuse, but in some cases stigma played a role.

Public meetings of LGBT advocacy groups and debates on the issue of rights for all persons regardless of sexual orientation or gender identity occurred without disruption or interference. An independent organization, LeGaBiBo (Lesbians, Gays, and Bisexuals of Botswana), has attempted to register as an NGO since 2009 to advocate for the rights of LGBT persons, but the government refused to register it on the basis that LeGaBiBo promoted an illegal activity. LeGaBiBo operated under the umbrella of the Botswana Network of Ethics on Law and HIV/AIDS (BONELA), which in 2011 filed a lawsuit challenging the government's decision not to register LeGaBiBo; however, it subsequently withdrew its lawsuit due to technical errors in its founding affidavit. In 2012 LeGaBiBo again applied for registration as an LGBT rights organization with the Registrar of Societies. The application was again denied on the same basis as previously. LeGaBiBo appealed the denial to the minister of home affairs, who also denied the application. In March LeGaBiBo again filed a lawsuit challenging the government's refusal to grant the organization legal status, this time on its own behalf and with the legal support of Unity Dow, one of the country's most respected human rights activists and jurists. The case was pending at year's end, with a High Court hearing expected in early 2014.

Other Societal Violence or Discrimination

Discrimination against persons with HIV/AIDS continued to be a problem, including in the workplace. The government funded community organizations that ran antidiscrimination and public awareness programs. BONELA continued to advocate for an HIV employment law to curb discrimination in the workplace.

Section 7. Worker Rights

a. Freedom of Association and the Right to Collective Bargaining

The law provides for the rights of workers, except police, military, and prison personnel, to form and join independent unions, to bargain collectively, and to strike, provided certain restrictions are observed. Police, military, and prison personnel are represented by employee associations, which serve as a means to communicate collective needs and concerns to their government employer. Union representatives reported that employee associations were generally not as effective as unions in resolving labor disputes. The law grants certain privileges (such as access to an employer's premises for purposes of recruiting members, holding meetings or representing workers, deduction of trade union dues, and recognition of trade union representation with regard to grievances) only to unions representing at least one-third of the employees in an enterprise. The law provides for certain restrictions that limit the right to organize. Trade unions that fail to meet some of the formal registration requirements are automatically dissolved and banned from carrying out union activities. The law does not afford protection to members of unregistered trade unions. The law also authorizes the registrar to inspect accounts, books, and documents of a trade union at "any reasonable time" and provides the minister of defense, justice, and security with the authority to inspect a trade union "whenever he considers it necessary in the public interest."

The law provides for collective bargaining only for unions that have enrolled one-third of a sector workforce. The law does not prohibit acts of interference by employers or employers' organizations in the establishment, functioning, or administration of trade unions. The law also permits an employer or employers' organization to apply to the government to withdraw the recognition granted to a trade union if it establishes that the trade union refuses to negotiate in good faith with the employer.

The law severely restricts the right to strike. All strikes are illegal unless compulsory arbitration procedures are first exhausted. The law prohibits sympathy strikes. Employees categorized as those in the "essential services," including the Bank of Botswana, railway services, health care, firefighting, military, transport services, telecommunications infrastructure, electricity, water, and sewage workers are not allowed to strike. In response to the 2011 public sector strike, the minister of labor and home affairs issued a regulation that added teachers, veterinarians, and diamond workers to the list of those providing essential services. The unions won a High Court case challenging the reclassification, but the government appealed the decision. The case was pending a decision by the Court of Appeals at year's end.

The law empowers the commissioner and the minister to refer a dispute in essential services to arbitration or to the industrial court for determination. Striking workers participating in an illegal strike may face dismissal.

Civil service disputes are referred to an ombudsman for resolution, and in general the ombudsman's decisions are made independently without government interference. Labor commissioners mediate private labor disputes and, if not resolved, they are sent to the Industrial Court. The time it took to resolve a labor dispute lasted between 11 months and five years.

While the law allows formally registered unions to conduct their activities without interference, members of nonregistered unions are not protected against antiunion discrimination. The law provides for protection against antiunion discrimination. Workers may not be fired for legal union-related activities. Dismissals may be appealed to civil courts or labor officers, which rarely ordered more than two months' severance pay. The law does not provide for reinstatement of workers, but a judge may order reinstatement if the firing is deemed to be related to union activities. The law does not provide protection to public employees' organizations from acts of interference by the public authorities in their establishment or administration.

Freedom of association was generally respected, although there were some restrictions on the right to collective bargaining. Workers exercised the right to form and join unions, and in general employers did not use hiring practices to avoid hiring workers with bargaining rights. The government, while seeking to expand the definition of essential services, generally protected the right to conduct union activities. In May 2012 the unions appealed to the ILO with complaints that included union freedom of assembly restrictions in the constitution, unlawful deregistration of the Botswana Federation of Public Sector Unions (BOFEPUSU), onerous balloting and meeting requirements for unions, improper categorization of "essential workers" to prohibit striking, and a lack of impartial mediation machinery. At year's end the ILO continued investigating these charges. Following the 2011 strikes, BOFEPUSU brought several cases before the courts, including the deregistration case, reduction of essential services workers, the government's lack of participation in bargaining councils, the government's withdrawal of benefits to some union members, and a challenge to the president's appointments to the industrial court. The cases were pending at year's end.

When the unions followed legal requirements of exhausting arbitration and notifying the government in advance of a planned strike, the government permitted the unions to strike and did not use force on strikers. Due to the strike requirements, however, many strikes were ruled illegal, and striking workers often faced risked of dismissal. Government employees in air traffic control services, the Botswana Vaccine Laboratory, electricity services, fire services, the Bank of Botswana, health services, veterinary services, the operation and maintenance of rail services, sewerage services, some transport and telecommunications services, and water services as well as teachers, and diamond workers are classified as essential workers prohibited from striking. In 2011 the government dismissed 2,844 public sector workers for strike activity, some of whom were eventually, selectively re-employed on less favorable terms and conditions.

The labor commissioners continued to be insufficient in number, resulting in two-year backlogs in resolving labor disputes. The government informed the ILO during the year that it recognized the need to have an independent dispute resolution mechanism and that the mechanism was to be included in the National Development Plan 10 (2009-16). No data concerning such program were available.

b. Prohibition of Forced or Compulsory Labor

The constitution and law prohibit all forms of forced and compulsory labor, including by children. While the law does not specifically prohibit trafficking in persons, it prohibits child prostitution and child trafficking. Civil society representatives reported that the government did not effectively enforce relevant laws, particularly in remote areas, mainly because a lack of sufficient staff and funding made it difficult for the government to send labor officers to enforce the law in remote areas. There were reports of forced child labor in cattle herding and in domestic servitude (see section 7.c.).

As part of an ILO-funded project, the children's rights NGO Childline reported it removed nine children from forced labor in agriculture between August 2010 and January 2012. The children's rights NGO Humana People to People Botswana, working separately on the same ILO project, reported it removed 268 children from agricultural labor between June 2010 and May 2012. It was unclear how many of the children in agricultural labor were in forced labor situations. Data on the number of victims removed from forced labor conditions were not available.

Government officials suggested that Zimbabweans may use the country as a transit point to move victims to South Africa.

Also see the Department of State's *Trafficking in Persons Report* at www.state.gov/j/tip.

c. Prohibition of Child Labor and Minimum Age for Employment

Children 14 years or older may be employed in light work that is "not harmful to [their] health and development" and is approved by a parent or guardian. The law provides that work shall not exceed six hours per day when a child is not in school and five hours when a child is in school. The law provides that a child should not "move anything so heavy as to be likely to endanger his physical development," work underground or at night, or engage in anything dangerous or immoral. The law prohibits the exploitation for labor or coercion into prostitution of adopted children.

The Ministry of Labor and Home Affairs is responsible for enforcing child labor laws and policies in all sectors; however, resources were too limited for effective oversight in remote areas. District and municipal councils have child welfare divisions, which are also responsible for enforcing child labor laws. Other involved government entities included offices with the Ministry of Education and the Ministry of Local Government. The Advisory Committee on Child Labor facilitated the oversight of child labor issues. It included representatives of various NGOs, government agencies, workers' federations, and employers' organizations and advised the government on the state of children three to four times during the year. The government supported and worked with partners to conduct workshops to raise awareness of child labor. The Department of Labor collaborated with the Department of Social Services to advocate against and raise awareness of exploitative child labor. Ministers continued to address public gatherings (referred to locally as "kgotla") cautioning against child labor.

In 2011 the Ministry of Labor and Home Affairs began work on a detailed classification of occupations deemed hazardous for children and conducted outreach events, including a weekly radio program, to spread awareness in rural areas. NGOs reported that the list was submitted to the cabinet in 2011 but remained unimplemented at year's end.

Despite the laws and policies designed to protect children from exploitation in the workplace, there were reports of child labor, mostly on subsistence-level cattle posts or farms.

According to the 2005-06 labor survey, slightly fewer than 38,000 children between the ages of seven and 17 were employed in 2006. Approximately half of those were under 14. More than 60 percent of employed children worked in agriculture, 20 percent in retail trade, and 4 percent in private homes. Two-thirds of employed children were working in rural villages. Children also worked as domestic laborers and in informal bars. Outside of supermarkets, children sometimes assisted truck drivers with unloading goods and carried bags for customers. Many orphans also left school to work as caregivers for sick relatives. Most employed children worked up to 28 hours per week.

Also see the Department of Labor's *Findings on the Worst Forms of Child Labor* at www.dol.gov/ilab/programs/ocft/tda.htm.

d. Acceptable Conditions of Work

According to June 2011 formal sector employment statistics from Statistics Botswana, the minimum hourly wage for most full-time labor in the private sector was 4.20 pula ($0.48). The minimum wage for domestic workers was two pula ($0.26) per hour, or approximately 16 pula ($2.05) per day. The minimum wage for workers in the agricultural sector was 445 pula ($50.95) per month, but the cost of feeding a worker who lived on the employer's premises could be deducted from the wages. According to the same survey, monthly average earnings were 4,339 pula ($513) for citizens, 13,055 pula ($1,537) for noncitizens, and 4,731 pula ($557) for all employees at the end of June 2011. The cabinet determined wage policy based on recommendations from the National Economic, Manpower, and Incomes Committee, which consists of representatives of the government, private sector, and Botswana Federation of Trade Unions. The Ministry of Labor and Home Affairs is responsible for enforcing the minimum wage, and each of the country's districts had at least one labor inspector.

The law permits a maximum 48-hour workweek, exclusive of overtime, which is payable at time-and-a-half. The law does not specifically outline rest periods or prohibit excessive compulsory overtime. The law prescribes 40-hour workweek for most modern private sector jobs and a 48-hour workweek for the public sector. The labor law also applies to farm and migrant workers. The Department of Labor had inspectors to oversee and enforce labor regulations. There are limited requirements for occupational safety. The law provides that workers who complain about hazardous conditions may not be fired. The government's ability to enforce its workplace safety legislation remained limited by inadequate staffing and unclear jurisdictions among different ministries.

The government generally enforced wage, hour, health, and safety requirements, but the number of labor inspectors was insufficient to inspect all workplaces. In 2012 the government conducted 1,701 labor inspections, finding 202 cases of unpaid overtime worked and 150 cases of payment below the minimum wage. The Ministry of Labor and Home Affairs conducted outreach events, including a weekly radio program, to spread awareness in rural areas.

Formal sector jobs generally paid well above minimum wage levels. The primary forms of compensation for labor in the informal sector were housing and food, particularly in the agricultural and domestic service areas. Pay in the informal sector was frequently below the minimum wage. Informal sector workers generally were covered by the same legal protections available to formal sector workers.

Foreign migrant workers were vulnerable to exploitative working conditions, mainly in domestic labor. Employers in the formal sector generally provided for worker safety.